Int:

I've never read the *Game of Thrones* books by George R. R. Martin.

There, I said it.

I've always wanted to, seriously. In fact, I've "started" the books a few times but could never get into them. It's not like I hate the genre: the *Lord of the Rings* series is among my lifelong favorites, and I read the series and prequels and appendices with much excitement. I've also enjoyed some of Robert Jordan's books. But I've never read *A Song of Ice and Fire*, the series of thick tomes upon which the HBO series **"Game of Thrones"** is based. But the popularity of the series—it seems to win a pile of Emmy's every year—has made me want to watch the show, but I hesitated. Won't I be "missing everything" if I without having first read the books?

Well, I decided to go the other direction: I would watch the shows without having read the books and enjoy them on their own, ignoring all the background details and differences pointed out by those helpful folks on the Internet. I understand that people who have read the books are interested in pointing out every difference, but do all those tiny details matter? While that might be interesting to those who read the books, it's completely irrelevant to the new viewer who just wants to enjoy the show.

Does the show hold up on its own, as a stand-alone work? I decided to find out.

So I started watching Season One on HBO. Five minutes into the first episode, I had questions—not questions about how the books related to the show, but questions ABOUT THE SHOW. Who are these White Walker guys? And the lady that plays Catelyn Stark—where have I seen her before?

But looking things up on the Internet didn't help—because "everyone" else has seen the show, it's impossible to avoid spoilers. And if you have season- or episode-specific questions, like I did, it's hard to find a spoiler-free source. Just in researching this book, I ran into several spoilers. If you're interested in watching all the seasons from the beginning with no spoilers, then you've been avoiding ALL talk of **Game of Thrones** since the show premiered in 2011. There's nothing worse than standing around a party covering your ears every time someone brings up House Stark, right?

I realized I needed a **Binge Guide**, a book that walks me through the show, episode by episode, providing useful and timely information and trivia about the EPISODE I WAS WATCHING at the time I was watching it. And no spoilers about any episodes to follow! Is that too much to ask? Well, apparently it was, because I couldn't find anything like that.

So I decided to write it. Enjoy!

How to Use This Binge Guide

This guide will walk you through **Season 5** of HBO's epic **Game of Thrones**. I designed this book to replicate the experience of watching a show with a knowledgeable friend, one who enjoys the show with you and interjects with occasional pieces of information and trivia, but studiously avoids any spoilers or hints about what's to come.

To Get Started:

☐ Buy this book.

☐ Queue up the first episode of the season

☐ Open the book to the first episode—but don't read ahead! "There be spoilers here."

☐ Start watching. I've broken up the episode narrative into sections.

☐ As you watch, refer to the relevant section.

☐ After each section, I have added any **relevant information on casting and characters, interesting quotes, goofs made during production, and any other notes** pertaining to that particular scene or series of scenes. In some cases, all of the scenes set at the same location are grouped under one header. If you start to read about something you haven't seen, STOP and go back to watching the show.

☐ Continue watching until the show is over.

☐ At the end of each episode, I offer my **critique** of the episode, along with more notes on the episode in general.

☐ I've also created something that might be helpful—**Game of Thrones** is a show for adults and therefore contains **scenes with graphic violence and nudity**. While it's impossible to note the profanities used, I've made a list of the most violent scenes in the episode, along with any nudity I noticed. I also included times, in case you are looking to skip past a particularly scene.

☐ At the end of the book, I will include a short summary of what happened during the season for each House with major players.

A strength of the **Game of Thrones** television show is the way it artfully introduces the new and seasoned alike to the fascinating and complicated world of Westeros and the Seven Kingdoms. And while GOT is an amazing show, I think many have avoided diving into for fear of missing something or being overwhelmed by trivia.

Should that keep you from watching one of the **greatest television shows** ever produced? I don't think so. The show stands on its own without the books because it provides a convincing and moving narrative of the rise and fall of the people and empires in the Westeros and beyond.

So dive in, root for your favorite character

or House, and enjoy!

One more note: For consistent naming of season and episode numbers, I use the internet's standard numbering system for television show episodes, but it can be a little confusing. You'll see numbers that look like "S01E12" - in this case "S01" stands for Season One and "E12" stands for Episode 12, so **S01E12** means the twelfth episode of season one.

Thanks, and if you enjoy this Guide, let me know. I'd love to hear from people who find this book interesting or helpful. I can be reached at **greg@gregenslen.com** or via my website at **gregenslen.com**. You can also send me feedback or report any typos or missing/contradictory information at the website. But please, no spoilers!

Enjoy!
Greg Enslen

Episode One – "The Wars to Come"

Episode Number: S05E01

Original Air Date: April 21, 2015

Time: 53 minutes

Opening Credits

The animated map during the credits shows several important locations: **King's Landing**, **The Eyrie**, **Winterfell**, the **Wall**, and, across the **Narrow Sea**, **Pentos** and **Meereen**.

Notes: This is first time since **S01E08** that the opening credits animation includes the **Eyrie**. This is first time we've seen Winterfell without smoke pouring out of it since **S02E10**, and it's now controlled by **House Bolton**, whose sigil is the Flayed Man.

This is first time since **S01E01** that the opening credits animation includes the city of **Pentos**.

King's Landing

Two girls walk through a forest, and one is worried about the other's father finding out. They find a hut and, inside, a witch who reputably can tell the future. The blonde girl asks for hers, but the witch needs a taste of her blood. Her future: she will wed the king, but a younger woman will cast her down. She will have three children and the king twenty, but none will be hers. "Gold will be their crowns," the witch says, then began laughing. The other girl pulls at the blonde, telling young Cersei Lannister they need to leave.

In the present, Cersei rides in a litter on her way to the Sept of Baelor to attend the funeral of her father, Tywin Lannister. Inside, Jaime Lannister, her brother and lover looks on Tywin's body. Jaime says they need to work together to keep what House Lannister has obtained, but she's furious at him—he freed their brother, Tyrion Lannister, who killed Tywin and then disappeared.

Grand Maester Pycelle follows Cersei, telling her she never trusted Lord Varys. She meets another cousin, **Lancel Lannister**, a cousin and a former lover of Cersei's, who is calling himself a Sparrow now, a follower of the Faith of the Seven. He asks her forgiveness for their "unnatural" relationship, and for giving Robert Baratheon too much wine during the boar hunt that led to his accidental death.

In bed, **Ser Loras Tyrell** spends time with his lover, **Olyvar**. His sister **Margaery** comes in, telling Loras they are late to see the king. Loras is happy—with Tywin dead, no one can force him to marry Cersei, but Margaery is dubious.

Notes: "Gold will be their crowns" means they will have blonde hair. The rest of her "future" comes true, including the king's 20 bastard children, among them Gendry. This is first flashback ever seen on Game of Thrones—every other scene from the last four seasons has either been present tense or glimpses of the future. According to the official HBO synopsis, the witch is named Maggy the Frog, although it's not mentioned during the episode.

Pentos

Tyrion Lannister is looking out the hole of his crate, seeing sailors and later, a city. The lid is removed, and he tumbles out to find **Lord Varys** holding a crowbar. Tyrion is bearded and weak and angry—he wants to know why he had to stay in the crate while they were on board the boat. Varys says he saved Tyrion's life, and letting him out was too dangerous. They then quickly discuss the logistics of Tyrion relieving himself while in the crate. They are at the home of Illyrio Mopatis, and Tyrion finds something to drink.

Later, they discuss why Varys set him free— and he did it for the Seven Kingdoms. Varys thinks Tyrion will be more useful alive for "the war to come," and looks to a time of peace. Varys is riding for Meereen to meet Daenerys Targaryen and wants Tyrion to come along.

Quotes: Lord Varys: "You have your father's instincts for politics and you have compassion." Tyrion Lannister: "Compassion. Yes. I killed my lover with my bare hands and I shot my own father with a crossbow." Lord Varys: "I never said you were perfect. The Seven Kingdoms need someone stronger than Tommen but gentler than Stannis. A monarch who could intimidate the High Lords and inspire the people. A ruler loved by millions, with a powerful army, and the right family name." Tyrion Lannister: "Good luck finding him." Lord Varys: "Who said anything about "him"?"

Notes: This is the first time we've seen the home of Illyrio Mopatis since **S01E01**.

Goofs: The scene shows Tyrion looking out the "hole" in his crate, but later it shows that there are several holes which should have been visible.

Meereen

In the east in the desert city of **Meereen**, slaves pull down the golden harpy idol atop a massive pyramid. It crashes to the ground far below, and one of the **Unsullied** smiles. He walks to a brothel and, once inside, pays one of the whores to sing to him. A person in a mask kills him.

Ser Barristan Selmy brings the mask to the mother of dragons, **Daenerys Targaryen** t, and tells her it was found by the body. She recognizes it as being from the **Sons of the Harpy**, a resistance group. Nearby, **Grey Worm**, **Mossador** and **Missandei** listen. She tells Grey Worm, the leader of the Unsullied army, to find those responsible.

Later, **Daario Naharis**, an adviser to Daenerys, walks the streets of the city. He is returning from another city, Yunkai, after putting down a rebellion and returning the city to Daenerys' control. They have now instituted a council made up of both former slaves and former slaveholders. They have one request—they would like the fighting pits reopened, where men may volunteer to fight each other for sport.

Later, in her chambers, she and Daario discuss his youth growing up in the fighting pits. He suggests she let the dragons out of captivity to frighten her enemies. She descends to the catacombs, where she has them locked away, but they frighten her.

Quotes: Daenerys Targaryen: "Angry snakes lash out. It makes chopping off their heads that much easier."

Notes: This is the first time that Daenerys' dragons **Viserion** and **Rhaegal** are mentioned by name.

Winterfell

At **Castle Black**, home of the **Night's Watch**, **Jon Snow** trains more recruits to fight. Nearby, **Samwell Tarly** and **Gilly** watch. **Alliser Thorne** and **Janos Slynt** discuss the training, and the fire priestess **Melisandre** tells Jon that the "king wants a word" with him. Taking the elevator to the top of the massive **Wall** that separates the Seven Kingdoms from the wild spaces to the north, Jon and Melisandre discuss the Lord of Light.

Atop the Wall, Jon talks to **King Stannis Baratheon** and his adviser, **Davos Seaworth** about **Winterfell**, a famous castle to the south and once home to House Stark. Jon grew up there, but it's controlled now by Roose Bolton, head of House Bolton and the person who killed Lord Eddard Stark, Jon's father. They also discuss Tywin Lannister, and Stannis says he's taking back the north and wants Roose Bolton dead. He's planning to incorporate the wildlings into his army, then give them lands south of the Wall when the war is over. Stannis wants Jon to convince Mance Raydar to pledge fealty to Stannis and House Baratheon—or Stannis will consider the wildlings as enemies.

Jon meets with **Mance Raydar**, the head of the wildlings and the man who successfully united 90 different clans in the north. Jon tries to convince him to join Stannis' army, but Mance won't bend the knee—he doesn't want to answer to anyone, even if it means being burned at the stake. Melisandre lights the bonfire and Mance burns. Jon Snow puts an arrow through his heart, killing him and ending the torment.

The Vale

In an area to the south known as the Vale, **Sansa Stark** and **Petyr Baelish** watch as **Robin**, the **Lord of the Vale**, learns how to fight with a sword. The young boy is awkward for his age and useless as a warrior. Baelish and Sansa leave in a wagon, traveling west. Nearby, **Brienne of Tarth** and **Pod**, her squire, are traveling to Castle Black, searching for Sansa Stark or her brother, Jon Snow. Brienne's' angry that Arya Stark got away. A wagon passes them—they don't know it, but it carries Sansa Stark and Baelish. Sansa wants to know where they are headed, and Baelish says somewhere so far away, the Lannisters won't be able to find her.

Critique:

Ah, Game of Thrones. I missed you. And though it looks like a few weeks have passed in the show since Tyrion was crated up in the last episode—nice beard, Imp—not much has happened since we were away. Sansa and Baelish are touring the Vale with Robin "The Terminator" Arryn—ha ha, just kidding. The kid will never be able to hold a sword. Really, all he can do is tell people he wants to see someone "fly."

Maybe after there's a new Lord of the Vale, Robin can just be in charge of the Moon Door.

Brienne is looking sad and defeated after losing track of Arya Stark, one of the two people in the entire country she was sent out to find and protect. Now, even if she manages to find Sansa and take her under her protection, she's still only be capable of achieving 50% of her task. I was never that great in school, but isn't 50% an "F?" For failing?

In the north, I was sad to see Mance burn—I liked him, and I respected what he did, bringing together all the northern clans. I think he took his eye off the ball. Does it really matter if he's working for Stannis or not? The WHOLE point of this is to get as many of his people south of the Wall as quickly as possible, right?

Remember, there's an ARMY OF DEAD PEOPLE coming. Can't we all just get along? I think Stannis' offer of lands south of the Wall for the wildlings was generous. Too bad Mance didn't agree.

Tywin's dead, and Cersei's moping around and snapping at people, so all is right with the world. It's great to see her brought down a few pegs, and now with Jaime and Lancel out of the picture, she's single and free to drink herself into an early grave.

And Daenerys. Oh boy, don't get me started on the story in the east. I mean, LITERALLY nothing has happened that I find in the slightest bit interesting since she took the slave baton thingy away from the dude in Astapor and then rained dragonfire down on him. God that was awesome. "Slaves, rise up and kill your masters!"

After that it's been more of the same or worse, more of the boring "I'm in charge now and here's all the boring administrative stuff I have to deal with now on a daily basis" stuff that makes me want to "fast forward" to the part where she starts using her dragons to burn stuff again.

Episode Notes:

The title of the episode refers to Lord Varys' and Mance Raydar's mentions of "the wars to come." This is the fifth king to die over the last five seasons, one per season: Season 1, Robert Baratheon; Season 2, Renly Baratheon; Season, Robb Stark; Season 4, Joffrey Baratheon; Season 5,

Mance Rayder.

Nudity and Violence:

Singing—One of the Unsullied tries to not take note of the topless whores in the streets (16:58). Inside, another whore gets naked for him (17:50) before his throat is slit (18:35)

Dorne—While Ser Loras Tyrell is in bed with his lover, Olyvar, we see Olyvar's butt (33:30) several times.

Fighting Pits—We see Daario's butt when they're discussing the fighting pits (40:25)

References:

Game of Thrones Wiki, several pages. http://gameofthrones.wikia.com/wiki/Game_of_T hrones_Wiki (accessed April 21, 2016)

HBO Game of Thrones Episode Synopsis. http://www.hbo.com/game-of-thrones/episodes/5/41-the-wars-to-come/synopsis.html (accessed April 21, 2016)

IMDB. http://www.imdb.com/title/tt3658012 (accessed

Game of Thrones: A Binge Guide to Season 5

April 21, 2016)

Episode Two – "The House of Black and White"

Episode Number: S05E02
Original Air Date: April 19, 2015
Time: 56 minutes

Opening Credits

The animated map during the credits shows several important locations: **King's Landing**, **The Eyrie**, **Winterfell**, the **Wall**, and, across the **Narrow Sea**, **Braavos** and **Meereen**.

Temple

Aboard a ship, Arya Stark arrives in the sprawling port city of Braavos, passing under the statue of the Titan. Ashore, the ship's captain takes her to **The House of Black and White**. A man answers the door but does not let her in, even after she shows him the coin given to her by Jaqen

H'ghar in **S02E10**. She sits on the steps and recites her kill list for several days, then throws it into the water and walks away.

Later, Arya's facing off against three thugs in the streets of Braavos when the man from the House of Black and White appears again and leads her to the temple. He changes faces and is **Jaqen H'ghar**—and invites her inside, telling her she must become no one.

Notes: Arya's kill list, started in **S02E04** in Harrenhal, now consists of Cersei...Walder Frey...The Mountain...Meryn Trant. Many of the other men on the list are dead, including King Joffrey, Polliver, The Tickler, Lorch, Rorge and The Hound. For some reason Ilyn Payne is off her list, even though he's the man who beheaded her father. Meryn Trant is on the list for killing Syrio Forel, as she assumes he was killed. Walder Frey is a new addition for killing her mother and brother.

Tavern

In a tavern, **Brienne of Tarth** and her squire **Pod** enjoy a warm meal and Pod is smitten with the serving girl. In the same tavern, **Sansa Stark** and **Petyr Baelish** discuss his new wedding proposal. Pod recognizes Baelish and tells Brienne, who approaches them and kneels to Sansa, pledging to protect her. But after Baelish explains her past failures in protecting King Renly and Catelyn Stark, Sansa dismisses her. Brienne leaves but Baelish has his guards chase them. Pod's horse throws him and Brienne rescues him, killing two of Petyr's men. They follow Sansa and Petyr on the East Road,

Notes: Sansa says her mother used to say "dark wings, dark words." This is the title of episode S03E02, when Robb and Catelyn Stark learn via a raven's message that Winterfell has been sacked.

Tyrell

In King's Landing, **Cersei Baratheon** shares with her brother, **Jaime Lannister**, news of a recent threat—she's received the necklace last worn by their daughter Myrcella in Dorne. House Tyrell is angry over the death of Prince Oberyn Tyrell in **S04E08**. Jaime says he'll travel to Dorne and bring her back. Cersei tells him to check the Water Gardens.

In Stokesworth, **Bronn** is avoiding listening to his betrothed **Lollys** prattle on and on about their approaching wedding—she has very specific ideas about what the wedding will entail. Bronn's more interested in talking about who will inherit the sprawling family estate. Jaime arrives to ask Bronn along on his mission to rescue his daughter from Dorne.

Back in King's Landing, the head of another dwarf is brought to Cersei, but it's not Tyrion. **Ser Meryn** escorts the hunters out and **Qyburn** keeps the head "for his work." At the Small Council, Cersei leads while adding Qyburn to the group. **Lord Mace Tyrel**l is now Master of Ships and Coin. Qyburn replaces Lord Varys as Master of Whisperers, and Cersei's uncle **Kevan** joins as Master of War, but he passes on the honor. Grand Maester Pycelle is annoyed that Qyburn is part of the Small Council.

The Water Gardens

In Dorne, **Ellaria Sand**, paramour to the slain Prince Oberyn Martell, meets with **Prince Doran**, Oberyn's brother. Doran is ill and confined to a wheeled chair. Ellaria wants him to go to war, saying the Sand Snakes also desire it.

Notes: These are the first scenes set in Dorne.

Tracked

In the east in the desert city of **Meereen**, **Daario Naharis** walks with **Grey Worm**, the leader of the Unsullied. The track a member of the Sons of the Harpy to his home and find him hiding in the wall. Later, **Daenerys Targaryen** listens to her advisers discuss the situation. **Ser Barristan Selmy** councils for mercy and a fair, public trial of the prisoner.

To the west, **Lord Varys** and **Tyrion Lannister** travel in secret via an enclosed wagon on the road to meet with Daenerys. Tyrion wants to walk but Varys says it's too dangerous: Cersei has offered a lordship to the person who brings her

Tyrion's head.

Later, the slave advising Daenerys takes the law into his own hands and kills the Son of the Harpy. He tells her he did what she could not. In a public show of her power, she orders the slave's execution. Drogon returns.

Quotes: Lord Varys: "You were quite good, you know. At ruling. During your brief tenure as Hand." Tyrion Lannister: "I didn't rule. I was a servant." Lord Varys: "Still, a man of talent." Tyrion Lannister: "Managed to kill a lot of people." Lord Varys: "Yes, but you show great promise in other areas as well."

Teacher

Shireen is teaching **Gilly** how to read while **Samwell Tarly** reads nearby. Gilly asks about Greyscale and says it killed two of her sisters and wonders who Shireen was cured. The Greyscale made them act like animals. Shireen's mother **Selyse** arrives and tells her to stay away from the wildlings.

King Stannis Baratheon chastises **Jon**

Snow for showing Mance Raydar mercy and killing him with an arrow while he was being burned alive. Stannis wants Jon to join him and offers to make him a Stark and **Lord of Winterfell**. Jon tells Samwell it's what he's always wanted, but he must refuse—he's a brother of the Night's Watch now. The brothers hold their election—it's between **Alliser Thorne** and **Denys Mallister**, but Samwell stands and throws a third name into the pot: Jon Snow. The vote is cast and Jon elected **Lord Commander of the Night's Watch**.

Quotes: Samwell Tarly: "Whilst Lord Janos was hiding with the women and children, Jon Snow was leading. Ser Alliser fought bravely, tis true. When he was wounded it was Jon who saved us. He took charge of the Wall's defense, he killed the Magnar of Thenns, he went north to deal with Mance Rayder, knowing it would've almost certainly meant his own death. Before that, he lead the mission to avenge Lord Commander Mormont. Mormont, himself, chose Jon to be his steward. He saw something in Jon and now we've all seen it to. He may be young but he's the commander we turned to when the night was darkest."

Notes: Old Maester Cressen taught Shireen how to read. He poisoned himself while trying to poison Melisandre in **S02E01**. They are electing the 998th Lord Commander of the Night's Watch.

Critique:

Plots are moving forward, with the most interesting being Arya's arrival in Braavos and her journey to the steps of The House of Black and White. I'm curious to see where this goes, and if she learns to put the order ahead of her own personal needs for revenge. I also find it interesting that her father inadvertently started her journey to Braavos by hiring a swordsman from that city—if she hadn't trained under Syrio Forel, then later mentions of the city of Braavos by the Faceless Man wouldn't have had the same impact.

Elsewhere, a new plot is launched to give Cersei and Jaime something to do now that Tywin is death, Tyrion is out of their reach and Cersei's wedding is canceled—she is worried about the safety of their daughter after receiving the necklace Myrcella was wearing. But if they were really planning on doing her harm, wouldn't they have sent a body part, as suggested by Ellaria? I'm glad Jaime and Bronn have a mission—they would both get bored pretty quickly. And it gives Cersei a break from throwing mean looks at Margaery.

In the east, yet another episode where Daenerys gets to deal with boring administrative stuff. Next episode, I bet she'll be working with the builders to go over the detailed plans for a new septic system, and maybe discuss starting a slave collar recycling program. Yawn.

And up in the north, Jon gets an offer and then another offer. I liked the "class president" style of voting, with people getting up and making speeches and then the old guy coming in at the last second with his vote. Why does he get to vote last, and so dramatically? Shouldn't his vote just go in the pot with the rest of them? Oh, and do they really have SO many extra pots lying around that they can afford to waste them like that? I would have had everyone put their chits in the pot, and then...poured them out onto the counter to count them. I mean, someone made that pot with their own little hands. Why are they being so mean to the pot maker? Maybe they didn't like that pot ALL ALONG and were just looking for an excuse...sorry, I mean a "reason" to break it.

Episode Notes:

The title of the episode refers to the building Arya Stark visits in Braavos, the headquarters of the Faceless Men.

Nudity and Violence:

Knights—Brienne rescues the little squire by killing two of Petyr's knights (15:10)

References:

Game of Thrones Wiki, several pages. http://gameofthrones.wikia.com/wiki/Game_of_T hrones_Wiki (accessed April 21, 2016)

HBO Game of Thrones Episode Synopsis. http://www.hbo.com/game-of-thrones/episodes/5/42-the-house-of-black-and-white/synopsis.html (accessed April 21, 2016)

IMDB.
http://www.imdb.com/title/tt3846626 (accessed April 21, 2016)

Episode Three – "High Sparrow"

Episode Number: S05E03
Original Air Date: April 26, 2015
Time: 60 minutes

Opening Credits

The animated map during the credits shows several important locations: **King's Landing**, **Moat Cailin**, **Winterfell**, the **Wall**, and, across the **Narrow Sea**, **Braavos** and **Meereen**.

Sweep Up

In **The House of Black and White**, **Arya** sweeps around those who worship the various idols of the Many-Faced God. Arya speaks with **Jaqen H'ghar.** She wants to learn how to be a Faceless Man, not sweep floors. Jaqen says there is only one god. A worshiper dies, and men come to take him away.

Later, a young woman enters Arya's

chambers and asks her who she is. When Arya says "no one," the woman strikes her repeatedly. Arya's about to use Needle, her sword, when Jaqen H'ghar enters. She says she was playing "the game of faces," but Jaqen says she's not ready: she's still wearing Arya Stark's clothes and carrying her things. Outside, she throws all of her possessions into the water, except for her sword, which she can't discard. Instead, she buries **Needle** under a rock near the beach.

Later, when she is sweeping, Jaqen leads her into a new area of the temple where they take the dead worshipers. She and the young woman undress the body, then washes it.

Wedding

In King's Landing, **King Tommen** weds **Margaery**. **Cersei Baratheon** is unhappy but there is nothing she can do about it. Later, and without haste, Margaery consummates the marriage with Tommen. Afterward, Margaery hints that his mother will always think of him as a child. "You'll always be her baby boy." The next day,

Tommen asks his mother is she misses Casterly Rock and suggests she might be happier there. Cersei visits Margaery, who hints that Cersei likes her wine "early in the day" and says she's exhausted from their wedding night, making it clear they've consummated the marriage.

At Petyr Baelish's brothel, the High Septon, a religious leader, is holding a mock ceremony with several nude women and **Olyvar** dressed as an old man. He chooses to worship the "maiden" and the "stranger," and Olyvar comments that he always chooses the maiden. "Sparrows" burst in, breaking up the "profane" ceremony and marched the High Septon naked through the streets. Later he goes before the Small Council and demands the "sparrows" and their leader, the **High Sparrow**, be punished. Cersei goes to meet this man and says she shares his disdain for hypocrisy— and has jailed the High Septon.

In Qyburn's laboratory, he kills a rat and is examining it when Cersei comes in with a message. She asks him to send it to Littlefinger at the Eyrie or wherever he is. The "thing" under the sheet on

Qyburn's table moves, and he answers "easy, friend."

Notes: This is the first we learn that Cersei and Littlefinger are working together and that she knows where he is. The thing under the sheet is most likely Ser Gregor "The Mountain" Clegane, or what's left of him—he was fatally poisoned in the "trial by combat" with Prince Oberyn Martell in **S04E08**, and Qyburn asked to care for him afterward.

Return to Winterfell

At the castle of Winterfell, repairs are underway to return the proud castle to its former glory—it was sacked some time ago after being capture by House Greyjoy and held for a short amount of time. Among those repairing Winterfell is **Reek**, a man formerly known at Theon Greyjoy. He's been tortured to the point of giving up his old identity and is now a manservant to the sadistic Ramsey Bolton. Theon grew up in this castle. He watches as they hang up the two flayed bodies of a man and a woman.

Inside, **Lord Roose Bolton** chastises his son **Ramsey**, saying they can't hold the North by terror along. Ramsey, charged with collecting taxes, says he flayed Lord Cerwyn and his wife and brother because they refused to pay, but their son, the new Lord Cerwyn, paid. Roose says their pact with Tywin Lannister is over, and it's up to them to defend the North on their own. Roose has arranged for a marriage that will guarantee them the North—Sansa Stark.

Nearby, **Sansa Stark** and **Petyr Baelish** approach Moat Cailin, and she guesses the reason, immediately protesting. Petyr explains that she must take her revenge for her family, and that means marrying a Bolton.

Following them at a distance is Brienne of Tarth and her squire Pod; they are watching over Sansa from afar, tasked with protecting her. Brienne is biding her time, waiting to step in and be of use. Later, they make camp and Brienne promises to train Pod in sword fighting and riding, then tells the tale of how Lord Renly saved her from an embarrassing situation.

Goofs: Not really a goof, but more just lodging a complaint—I don't care what kind of state of disrepair the fortress of Winterfell was it, it wouldn't just sit empty for so long. Winterfell is famous, and someone would have come along and moved in if it were just sitting empty, implying that House Bolton probably had possession of it this whole time. But if that's true, why didn't the sigil change until **S05E01**?

Notes: This is the first time we've seen Winterfell, except from a distance, since the castle was sacked in **S02E10**.

Castle Black

King Stannis Baratheon and his adviser, **Davos Seaworth**, speak to **Lord Commander of the Night's Watch Jon Snow**. Jon says he must stay at the Wall and cannot ride with Stannis and Davos to take back Winterfell or bring the war to King's Landing. Later, Jon holds his first meeting as Lord Commander. He names **Alliser Thorne** First Ranger, then tasks **Janos Slynt** with overseeing the repair of Greyguard, one of the ruined castles along the Wall, but he refuses several times, leaving Jon no choice but to discipline him. Even after Slynt changes his mind and offers to do as he is told, Jon executes him.

Quotes: Jon Snow: "I heard it was best to keep your enemies close." Stannis Baratheon: "Whoever said that didn't have many enemies."

Sansa

Petyr Baelish and Sansa Stark arrive at Winterfell, and she meets Roose and Ramsey Bolton. Miranda, a female friend of Ramsey's, is unhappy with Sansa's arrival. A woman shows Lady Stark to her chambers, and then says "the North remembers."

Later she walks through the yard at Winterfell and Theon sees her and avoids her. Ramsey thanks Petyr for setting up the match, and then Petyr tells Roose that Sansa is still a virgin and, "by the law," she is no man's wife. Bolton is concerned that the Lannisters will be angry at the union, but Baelish is unconcerned, even after receiving an urgent message from Cersei.

Notes: This is the first time Sansa has been back to her childhood home since she left with her father, Arya, and the king's entourage in **S01E02**.

Volantis

Across the Narrow Sea, **Lord Varys** and **Tyrion Lannister** travel in secret via an enclosed wagon on the road to meet with Daenerys. Tyrion is bored and wants to get out when they reach Volantis. In the market, they see a fire priestess talking about the Dragon Queen. After she looks at Tyrion, they repair to a brothel and drink. And, by coincidence, enjoying drinks in the same brothel is **Jorah Mormont**. He spots Tyrion and kidnaps him. "I'm taking you to the queen."

Quotes: Tyrion Lannister: "I will not be of any use to Daenerys Targaryen if I lose my mind. I can't remember the last face I saw that wasn't yours." Lord Varys: "It's a perfectly good face."

Notes: Lady Talisa Maegyr, bride of Robb Stark before she was murdered, was from Volantis. Tyrion mentions that the only "red priest" they had in Westeros was Thoros of Myr. We last saw Thoros in **S03E07** when he gave Gendry, the armorers apprentice, to Melisandre. When Tyrion says "I need to speak to someone with hair" in the brothel, he's making a joke about speaking to anyone who isn't Lord Varys, who is bald.

--------------------------------------—

Critique:

Arya's story gets a big boost as she finally arrived in Braavos last episode and now we start to learn the inner workings of The House of Black and White. The religion, so far, involves her doing a LOT of sweeping and then throwing away her money and clothes. As she and the other woman seem to be the only people working in the temple, I hope they keep up with their sweeping or it's going to get dirty soon. I do enjoy how the Faceless never seem to use "I" or "me" and only refer to themselves as "this one." Nifty.

Oh, and then Sansa Stark's story takes a nose-dive as they manage to marry her to the least likable person in the entire nation of Westeros.

Ramsey is evil and I fear the only thing that will keep poor Sansa alive is her name—of course, that doesn't mean he can't have LOTS of Joffrey-style fun with her. Talk about out of the frying pan…Joffrey was bad because he was a sadist who was also the king, so he could get away with anything.

This guy is worse because he is so much more imaginative in coming up with new ways to torture people. Let's see, so far he's: castrated Theon after teasing him with two naked women; tricked Theon into thinking he was escaping only to lead him back into captivity; chased a woman through the woods and then let his two dogs eat her; and flayed an unknown number of people alive.

King Tommen marries Margaery and she very nearly raced him into bed so they could consummate the marriage. I GUARANTEE you they didn't stop for wine or pie of any sort between the Sept of Baelor and the wedding bed—hell, Margaery was probably already stripping off her clothes before they even got into the King's private chambers. Third time's the charm! Did she consummate the marriage to Renly? I'm not sure—all I know is this is her third try at being a queen and dammit she's going to make it happen. You have to admire her for that "stick to it" attitude of hers.

Episode Notes:

The title of the episode refers to the leader of the "sparrows."

Nudity and Violence:

Flayed—The flayed bodies put on display at Winterfell are nasty (14:30)

Headless—Jon Snow decapitates Janos Slynt and it's pretty pretty gross (42:00)

The Seven—Boobs and butts aplenty, along with some frontal nudity from the whores during their weird "religious" orgy thingy at the brothel (42:10). Later, the High Septon is marched naked through the streets (43:23)

Mother of Dragons—Varys and Tyrion visit a brothel in Volantis and we see "Daenerys" naked (56:50)

References:

Game of Thrones Wiki, several pages. http://gameofthrones.wikia.com/wiki/Game_of_Thrones_Wiki (accessed April 21, 2016)

HBO Game of Thrones Episode Synopsis. http://www.hbo.com/game-of-thrones/episodes/5/43-high-sparrow/synopsis.html (accessed April 21, 2016)

IMDB. http://www.imdb.com/title/tt3866836 (accessed April 21, 2016)

Episode Four – "Sons of the Harpy"

Episode Number: S05E04
Original Air Date: May 3, 2015
Time: 51 minutes

Opening Credits

The animated map during the credits shows several important locations: **King's Landing**, **Winterfell**, the **Wall**, and, across the **Narrow Sea**, **Braavos** and **Meereen**.

Notes: This is first time the opening credits animation has gone directly from King's Landing to Winterfell.

Volantis

Jorah Mormont steals a boat and throws a tied-up **Tyrion Lannister** in the back, setting sail. Later they talk and Tyrion's pleased to find out they're going to see Daenerys Targaryen—he tells Jorah he was on his way to see her anyway. Tyrion was worried Jorah was taking him back to Cersei, then puts the clues together and figures out his captor is Jorah Mormont, and guesses he's bringing Daenerys a "prize" to get back into her good graces.

Tarth

Jaime Lannister asks a deck hand if they're sailing past Estermont, but is told they're passing Tarth, the Sapphire Isle. Below decks, **Bronn** wonders why they're sailing on a merchant ship, and Jaime says they're sailing to Oldtown and will row to Dorne. Bronn's been there before and isn't keen on kidnapping anyone, and wonders why Jaime is taking this on.

Later, Bronn and Jaime cross the water to Dorne and are accosted by four Dornish men on horseback. Bronn kills three while Jaime fights one and learns a new strategy—he catches the man's sword with his golden hand.

On the beach, **Ellaria Sand** rides her horse to meet the **Sand Snakes: Nym, Obara,** and **Tyene.** They want to know if Dorne is going to war with the Lannisters, but Ellaria says they must ngeberyn alone. They have the ship captain buried up to his neck in the sand—he told them that he smuggled Jaime Lannister ashore recently. Ellaria realizes he's come for Myrcella,

Characters: Obara Sand is played by Oscar-nominated actress **Keisha Castle-Hughes**, best known for her roles in **Whale Rider** and **Star Wars Episode III - Revenge of the Sith**.

Quotes: Ellaria: "You must choose. Doran's way and peace, or my way and war."

Notes: Brienne is from the island of Tarth.

King's Landing

Lord Mace Tyrell, the Master of Coin, has some bad news for the other members of the Small Council, Jorah Mormont. including **Cersei**, **Qyburn**, and **Grand Maester Pycelle**: the **Iron Bank of Braavos** has called in one-tenth of what the crown owes. House Tyrell offers to front the money, to be paid back by the realm. Cersei sends him to Braavos to negotiate directly with the Iron Bank. In her office, Cersei meets with the **High Sparrow**. She offers to arm his followers, creating the **Faith Militant**.

In the streets, the Sparrows destroy barrels of alcohol, raid brothels and destroy shop stalls, all while the city guard looks the other way. A group of Sparrows led by **Lancel Lannister** arrests Ser **Loras Tyrell** for breaking the "laws of gods and men." When she learns about it, **Queen Margaery** is furious, telling the king that this is Cersei's revenge. She suggests he speak to the High Sparrow about it, but he's denied entry to the Sept of Baelor.

Castle Black

The **Night's Watch** trains while **King Stannis Baratheon** and his wife, **Selyse**, watch. They discuss **Jon Snow, Lord Commander**. She apologizes for not giving him any sons, only one deformed daughter, **Shireen**. **Melisandre** joins them and tells Selyse that Shireen is special—the king's blood flows through her. Stannis is marching on Winterfell soon, ahead of the snows. In his office, Jon Snow sends out letters to area lords for supplies and men, including Roose Bolton. Melisandre enters, telling him he should travel with them to Winterfell and then exposing herself to him, but he passes.

Shireen visits Stannis' rooms and asks if he's ashamed of her. He tells her how she got Greyscale—he bought a doll from a visiting vendor from Dorne, and she pressed it to her face, becoming infected. Stannis tried many healers until he found one who could heal her.

Winterfell

Sansa Stark is praying in the crypts below Winterfell when she's joined by **Petyr Baelish**, who is returning to King's Landing. Sansa doesn't want to be alone with the Boltons, but Petyr has news: Stannis Baratheon will be marching on Winterfell any day. Once he liberates the North, Stannis will rally the local lords and march south.

Notes: This is the first time we've seen the crypts below Winterfell since Bran and Rickon Stark were down here with Osha and Hodor, hiding from the Greyjoys. Maester Luwin discovered them hiding in **S02E08** before he was killed and the castle sacked. And the feather that Sansa picks up off the ground is likely the same one placed by King Robert Baratheon when he visited Lyanna Stark's statue in **S01E01**.

Meereen

In Meereen, the **Sons of the Harpy** attack a brothel, slitting the throats of the visiting men. A group of Unsullied led by **Grey Worm** give chase and are trapped. **Ser Barristan** joins them and both fall.

Critique:

Well, what to say? Not a lot happens on this episode, which is probably a good thing. There are so many plots to keep track of, I'm glad to see that they're making progress on some of them.

Lots of boats this episode: Jorah and Tyrion on a boat headed to Meereen, Jaime and Bronn on another boat headed to Dorne. Cersei insists that Lord Mace Tyrell get on a boat and travel to Braavos to personally negotiate with the Iron Bank for an extension on their debt.

The Sparrows remind me of the Spanish Inquisition ("Nobody expects the Spanish Inquisition!") or some crazy religious cult who are ready to get out there and stamp out fun in the world. Good job, guys! No more wine or whores. And....now King's Landing's economy comes to a grinding halt. Great.

Sansa, Sansa, Sansa. Really? They are House Bolton and their sigil is a Flayed Man. FLAYED MAN. Get it? You are digging yourself a hole girl. I think I know where this is going, and I can only hope that Reek turns back into Theon Greyjoy before it's too late.

I'm frustrated that we're four episodes into the fifth season and we still haven't learned anything about Bran Stark or that crazy lake full of skeletons. Or the dude who likes to live in the roots of an old tree and hang out with a weird bird and some freaky looking little girl. I hope they made camp and set up a fire and got comfortable, because it looks like it has been weeks in Westeros before we get back to them.

Episode Notes:

The title of the episode refers to the group of men fighting back against Daenerys' control of Meereen.

Nudity and Violence:

Sparrows—When the sparrows raid a brothel, we see several completely naked woman (11:38). And when the sparrows catch two men in the act, we see them naked as well (12:25). Also, Lancel Lannister has a bloody symbol of the seven carved into his forehead (12:45)

Surprise—Melisandre does that thing she does where she's talking to someone with highborn blood and then opens up her coat (21:25).

Snakes—When the Sand Snake spears the dude through the head, there's a bloody spray (40:30)

Sons—The Sons of the Harpy attack a brothel (46:30). Later the Unsullied and Barristan battle them and much blood is spilt (47:15)

References:

Game of Thrones Wiki, several pages. http://gameofthrones.wikia.com/wiki/Game_of_T hrones_Wiki (accessed April 21, 2016)

HBO Game of Thrones Episode Synopsis. http://www.hbo.com/game-of-thrones/episodes/5/44-sons-of-the-harpy/synopsis.html (accessed April 21, 2016)

IMDB. http://www.imdb.com/title/tt3866838 (accessed April 21, 2016)

Episode Five – "Kill the Boy"

Episode Number: S05E05

Original Air Date: May 10, 2015

Time: 57 minutes

Opening Credits

The animated map during the credits shows several important locations: **King's Landing**, **Winterfell**, the **Wall;** across the **Narrow Sea**, **Braavos** and **Meereen;** and far to the south, **Dorne**.

Notes: This is first time the opening credits animation has featured Dorne.

Selmy

Missandei sits by the bedside of **Grey Worm**, the injured leader of the **Unsullied**. In the main hall of the pyramid, **Ser Barristan Sully** lies in state. She orders the leaders of all the great Meereen families, including **Hizdahr zo Loraq**, rounded up and taken to the catacombs, where she gives one to her dragons while the others watch. Later, after discussing it with Missandei, **Daenerys** apologizes to Hizdahr zo Loraq and says they can reopen the fighting pits to free men only—and that she will take him as a husband to solidify her hold on Meereen.

Sacrilege

Jon Snow goes to **Maester Aemon** for advice, then makes a proposition to **Tormund**—peace. Jon wants Tormund and the rest of the wildlings to come south of the Wall before it's too late. Tormund agrees, but only if Jon goes with him. Jon announces it to the **Night's Watch**, but they're not keen on the idea—for 8,000 years, they've been fighting to keep anything and everything north of the Wall. Letting the wildlings through to settle northern lands is sacrilege. **King Stannis Baratheon** and **Davos Seaworth** watch as the other Night's Watch leaders argue with Jon, but he has a good retort: "We can let them through now, or we can fight them after they join the Army of the Dead."

In the library at Castle Black, **Samwell Tarly** is reading when King Stannis comes in to ask him about the dragonglass. Stannis says they have it on Dragonstone as well, and Samwell says daggers made of it can defeat the White Walkers. Stannis goes to tell Davos to prepare to move out, and that they're bringing **Melisandre**, **Selyse** and **Shireen** with them. In the morning, Stannis and his army ride out into the growing cold to march on Winterfell.

Quotes: Bowen Marsh: "Let them die. Less enemies for us." Stannis Baratheon: "Fewer." Davos Seaworth: "What?" Stannis Baratheon: "Nothing."

Notes: The whole "Less" vs. "Fewer" lesson in grammar is a repeat of the same conversation Stannis had with Davos over having "fewer" fingernails to clean in **S02E04**.

Stakeout

Brienne of Tarth and **Pod** are keeping an eye on Winterfell from a nearby inn. Pod wonders if Sansa is safe inside Winterfell, but Brienne reminds him that the Boltons murdered her brother and mother.

In Winterfell, **Ramsey Bolton** and his lover **Myranda** discuss his upcoming marriage to Sansa Stark while they're completely naked. And **Sansa Stark** gets a visitor, who lets her know that she has friends and "isn't alone" and tells her to light a candle in the broken tower if she's in trouble.

While visiting the broken tower, Myranda introduces herself and leads Sansa to the kennels. Sansa is worried but goes inside and finds **Theon Greyjoy** in one of the stalls. He tells her she shouldn't be there. Later, "Reek" tells Ramsey that Lady Sansa visited him in the kennels. Ramsey takes his hand and forgives him.

Later at dinner, Ramsey makes Reek apologize for killing Sansa's two younger brothers, and then Reese Bolton has some news—his new wife Wanda is pregnant. Afterward, the Boltons discuss Ramsey's mother and then talk strategy for the coming war: Stannis will be moving south soon, arriving at Winterfell.

Quotes: Ramsey Bolton: "That was getting

very tense."

Notes: the abandoned broken tower is the one Cersei and Jaime used for their secret rendezvous—and the tower Bran fell from—in **S01E01**. And Ramsey is the result of twisted incident: the miller had married without Reese's consent, so he had the miller hung and then raped his wife under the tree where the man swung.

Sailing

Jorah Mormont guides his stolen boat across the water. It carries a tied-up **Tyrion Lannister** in the back—Jorah is bringing the Imp to Daenerys as a "prize" to get back into her good graces. Tyrion recognizes the route ahead; Jorah is taking him to Meereen via **Valyria**. Tyrion says "the Doom still rules Valyria," and asks Jorah if he's afraid of the "demons and flames." They sail through the ruins of a beautiful city, and Tyrion says for thousands of years, the Valyrians were the best in the world at almost everything. They recite a poem together about the fall of Valyria just before **Drogon** flies over and disappears. Tyrion has never seen a dragon before.

Stone men attack the boat, men afflicted with Greyscale, which is said to turn a man feral. Jorah fights the off but Tyrion falls into the water, his hands still bound. A stone man drags him down into the water. Later, Tyrion awakens on a beach to find Jorah standing over him. Jorah goes to find wood to make a fire and looks at his arm—he's been infected with Greyscale.

Quotes: Tyrion Lannister: "The Smoking Sea. How many centuries before we learn how to build cities like this again? Thousands of years the Valyrians were the best in the world at almost everything. And then…" Jorah Mormont: "And then they weren't." Tyrion Lannister: "And then they weren't. 'They held each other close and turned their backs upon the end. The hills that split asunder and the black that ate the skies; The flames that shot so high and hot that even dragons burned; Would never be the final sights that fell upon their eyes. A fly upon a wall, the waves the sea wind whipped and churned—'" Jorah Mormont: "'The city of a thousand years, and all that men had learned; The Doom consumed it all alike, and neither of them turned.'" Tyrion Lannister: "I would clap."

Notes: In **S05E04**, Stannis mentions that he hired healers from half the world until he found a way to stop the disease in his daughter Shireen.

Critique:

Our first glimpses of the lost civilization of Valyria are fascinating, with the ruins buildings and aqueducts—and the Stone Men who attack Tyrion and Jorah. I love the idea that there have been civilizations around for thousands of years in Westeros and that some of them have fallen. Valyria is surrounded by legends and myth, including the tales of destruction by the "Doom." Tyrion and Jorah are clearly wary of passing through the area, and Jorah mentions that even pirates are afraid to go there.

Sansa figures out that Ramsey is a psycho when he trots out the ex-Theon Greyjoy as his new pet. Ramsey's father even calls Theon a "creature" and isn't happy with what his son has done to the eldest son of Greyjoy. Just think about that—Roose Bolton flays people all the time, and he thinks what Ramsey's done is going too far. Wow.

Again, the story in Meereen with Daenerys and her tenuous hold on the city moves along at it's standard breakneck glacial speed. This episode Daenerys makes a decision and then changes her mind about the decision (again) and Grey Worm...wakes up. Stop the presses! I can't keep up with all the changes. It's like on that old soap opera Santa Barbara when stuff happened BETWEEN the episodes and you had to figure out what the characters were talking about like you missed a show or something. This is just like that, except opposite.

I'm starting to hate the Faith Militant—they remind me of a bunch of angry Mormons or Muslims forcing their religion on other people. I don't have a problem with people following a religion, but forcing other people to "believe" what you believe has been path to persecution for centuries, at least on this planet. Maybe they'll figure it out on/in Westeros. That reminds me—is Westeros like an alternate Earth? They seem to have all the same species we have: last episode, Bronn and Jaime were comparing sharks and dolphins and the animal names were spelled the same. If they were calling them "shaarks" and "dolfins" as George R. R. Martin seems to like, I could see a difference, but now I'm even more curious. I like the High Sparrow but I have a feeling Cersei's offer to arm his people is going to backfire on her in some way.

Episode Notes:

The title of the episode refers to the Maester Aemon's advice to Jon Snow: kill the Boy, and let the man be born. He means it's time for Jon to grow up and take charge.

Nudity and Violence:

Going Dutch—The dragons tear a dude apart and the body parts fly (7:25)

Window Seat—Oh, it's just Myranda,

staring out the window, naked (20:30) and then Psycho McPsycho joins her so great we get to see his butt (21:20), which is attached to a psycho. Of course, when they fight, we see her womanhood when she turns around (21:45)

References:

Game of Thrones Wiki, several pages. http://gameofthrones.wikia.com/wiki/Game_of_T hrones_Wiki (accessed April 22, 2016)

HBO Game of Thrones Episode Synopsis. http://www.hbo.com/game-of-thrones/episodes/5/45-kill-the-boy/synopsis.html (accessed April 22, 2016)

IMDB. http://www.imdb.com/title/tt3866840 (accessed April 22, 2016)

Episode Six – "Unbowed, Unbent, Unbroken"

Episode Number: S05E06

Original Air Date: May 17, 2015

Time: 54 minutes

Opening Credits

The animated map during the credits shows several important locations: **King's Landing**, **Winterfell**, the **Wall;** across the **Narrow Sea**, **Braavos** and **Meereen;** and far to the south, **Dorne**.

Sickly

In **The House of Black and White**, **Arya** washes the body of a dead worshiper. When she is done, two men come and take the body away. The Waif, the other young woman in the temple, comes in and tells Arya to get to work, but Arya refuses—she wants to know what's going on. The Waif says she's from Westeros and highborn but her stepmother tried to poison her. She sought help from the Faceless Men, who killed her stepmother, and the young woman has served them ever since. Arya smiles, but then the woman asks—was that all true, or a lie? In her bed, **Jaqen H'ghar** asks her who she is and then slaps her every time she says something true from her past.

She scrubs the floor of the temple as a man brings in his sickly daughter—he has nowhere else to go. His daughter suffers and he's been to every healer and is out of money. Arya lies and says she was sickly once as well and her father brought her in to be healed. She gives her the healing waters, killing her with mercy as Jaqen H'ghar watches.

Later, she washes the girl's body and Jaqen leads her deeper into the temple. She finds a huge room called the "**Hall of Faces**," with massive stone columns, each decorated with the faces of the dead and the living.

Notes: The official synopsis calls the other young woman in the House of Black and White the

"Waif, so we'll use it here although it's not yet been mentioned on the show. And they call the room with all the heads the "Hall of Faces.""

Shoreline

Jorah Mormont and **Tyrion Lannister** make their way along a shore. Jorah is taking him to Meereen. Tyrion is hungry and irritable from lack of wine, and Jorah asks him if he ever shuts up, then asks how he ended up in a brothel in Volantis. Tyrion says he killed his father and is on the run, then mentions he met Lord Commander Jeor Mormont, Jorah's father, and admired him. "We shall never see his like again."

Jorah didn't know his father had been killed by mutineers from the Night's Watch. They are captured by slavers and taken aboard their ship after Tyrion successfully negotiates for their lives.

Sparrows

Petyr "Littlefinger" Baelish returns to find **King's Landing** under the watchful eye of "Brother" **Lancel Lannister** and the **Faith**

Militant, armed followers of the **High Sparrow**. He meets with Cersei, mother of the king, and wonders if it was a good idea to arm the Faith Militant or stand by while they arrested Ser Loras Tyrell. She asks if the Lords of the Vale will fight for Westeros, and Petyr assures her that he's always counseled loyalty to the throne.

Petyr also tells her that he's found Sansa Stark, alive and well in Winterfell in the company of House Bolton. He says that Bolton plans to marry Sansa to his eldest, but at the same time, Stannis marches on Winterfell.

Petyr suggests patience, allowing them to fight each other and weakening both Houses. Cersei doesn't have the forces to take Winterfell from the weakened victor, and Baelish offers to take it with the Lords of the Vale—if she names him Warden of the North.

Lady Olenna of House Tyrell, Margaery's grandmother, arrives to meet with **Margaery**, who is worried about her imprisoned brother Ser Loras Tyrell. Olenna meets with Cersei, who makes her wait. They discuss Loras and the future of the Lannister-Tyrell alliance, trading bitter words. Later at an "inquest" for Loras, the **High Sparrow** grills him about his relationship with Renly Baratheon, then questions the Queen herself. They bring in Olyvar, one of Loras' lovers, who testifies that he and Loras had a relationship. He proves his testimony by identifying a birthmark. Loras and the queen are both arrested.

Quotes: Lady Olenna: "If they arrested all the pillow biters in King's Landing, there'd be no room left in the dungeons for anyone else."

Goofs: Loras is charged with deviant behavior after Olyvar mentions his birthmark. But, as his squire, he would have helped Loras dress and had many opportunities to see his birthmark without them being intimate.

Notes: Baelish is clearly setting up a fight between House Lannister and House Bolton. She says Roose Bolton is Warden of the North by the grace of Tywin, his reward for "stabbing his own king in the heart." Cersei makes Lady Olenna wait while writing a letter, the same thing her father used to do to people to make them uncomfortable.

Cersei calls Olenna the **Queen of Thorns**.

Sand Snakes

In the **Water Gardens of Dorne**, **Myrcella Lannister** and **Trystane Martell** discuss getting married once they have the blessing of **Prince Doran Martell**, who watches from above. He approves of the match but is worried for their safety. Nearby, **Ser Jaime Lannister** and **Bronn** make their way across the countryside of Dorne on horseback, disguised as Dornish soldiers in head scarves. In the distance they see the Water Gardens and move into the city.

The **Sand Snakes** pledge their vengeance for Oberyn and go into the Water Gardens just as Jaime and Bronn enter, all searching for Myrcella. Jaime finds her kissing Trystane, and Myrcella is surprised to see him so far from King's Landing. Trystane lunges at Bronn, who knocks him out. Jaime says they have to leave immediately as the Sand Snakes attack Jaime and Bronn. One of the Sand Snakes makes off with Myrcella as Prince Doran's guards arrive. Obara Sand, one of the Sand

Snakes and daughter of Oberyn Martell, says she is fighting for Dorne. They are all captured, along with **Ellaria Sand**.

Quotes: Bronn: "Once we've got the princess, then what?" Jaime Lannister: "I like to improvise." Bronn: "That explains the golden hand."

Sansa

In Winterfell, **Sansa Stark** is visited by **Myranda**, who offers to draw her a bath. Myranda is jealous of her beauty and tells Sansa to be careful of Ramsey's jealousy while she washes her hair. She tells her that Ramsey hunted Tansy and let the dogs at her body.

Sansa finishes dressing and **Theon** comes to escort her to the **Godswood**. She refuses to take his arm—she's still furious that he "killed" her brothers, Bran and Rickon Stark. Outside in the snow, they complete the ceremony under the weirwood tree and Lady Sana and Ramsey are married. In his room, **Ramsey** rapes Sansa Stark, taking her virginity while making Theon watch helpless in the corner.

Quotes: Ramsey Bolton: "You've known Sansa since she was a girl. Now watch her become a woman."

Notes: Kyra, Violet, and Tansy are all mentioned by Myranda as Ramsey's past lovers. Tansy was the woman Ramsey and Myranda hunted through the woods and fed to the dogs in **S04E02**. After they are married, Ramsey asks Sansa if she's lying about being a virgin, saying "lying to your husband on his wedding night, that would be a bad way to start a marriage." Then he rapes her.

Critique:

Ah, the "rape episode." I'd heard about this episode in pop culture, just like I'd heard about the Red Wedding, and I was dreading it, of course. And while critics have decried this episode as misogynistic, I'd push back on that—the whole show is misogynistic, as is the era depicted. It's also incredibly violent, with rich and poor, young and old people of all creeds and races getting murdered in the most violent fashions.

And, on this fictional show, people are mean to each other, and use naughty words. They have hobbies that I don't share and torture others for sport. Sometimes perfectly nice people have their heads chopped off and stuck on sharp sticks and used for decoration. I'm not saying what happened to Sansa Stark is good or bad—it's all fiction, remember, and part of a larger story—but it's meant to make us angry. For me, it made me glad to live in a world where this type of thing is seen as wrong and bad. Knowing so many people were disheartened by the abuse of a fictional character gives me hope. Maybe we, as a species, are moving in the right direction.

But the knee-jerk reaction by some, who want to protest the show or call for it to be taken off the air, is the wrong reaction, I think. While the subject matter is upsetting, I would far prefer to be discussing the rape of a fictional character than the rape of a real person. And, on that, I think we can

77

all agree.

Elsewhere, things seem less important, don't they? After thinking about Sansa and her predicament, worrying about Tyrion and Jorah getting enslaved or Jaime and Bronn fighting the Sand Snakes just didn't seem as important. And they should—yes, Sansa is raped, one of our favorite characters. But Tyrion was nearly killed, and Jaime and Bronn were captured. Those are bad things as well, and in a fictional world where bad things happen all the time, I'll have to chalk up this episode to just more of the same.

Episode Notes:

According to IMDB, the title of the episode refers to the words of House Martell although they are not mentioned during the episode. This episode, like the Red Wedding and Joffrey's assassination, features no music over the final credits.

Nudity and Violence:

Raped—Sansa is raped by Ramsey Bolton.

No nudity is involved, but it is a very violent, heart-wrenching scene (53:30)

References:

Game of Thrones Wiki, several pages. http://gameofthrones.wikia.com/wiki/Game_of_Thrones_Wiki (accessed April 22, 2016)

HBO Game of Thrones Episode Synopsis. http://www.hbo.com/game-of-thrones/episodes/5/46-unbowed-unbent-unbroken/synopsis.html (accessed April 22, 2016)

IMDB. http://www.imdb.com/title/tt3866842 (accessed April 22, 2016)

Episode Seven – "The Gift"

Episode Number: S05E07
Original Air Date: May 24, 2015
Time: 59 minutes

Opening Credits

The animated map during the credits shows several important locations: **King's Landing**, **Winterfell**, the **Wall;** across the **Narrow Sea**, **Braavos** and **Meereen;** and far to the south, **Dorne**.

The Night's Watch

Alliser Thorne and the other members of the **Night's Watch** watch as **Jon Snow** orders **Tormund**, the leader of the wildlings, freed from his chains. Jon is traveling with him north to gather the wildlings and send them to safety south of the Wall. Jon gives command of **Castle Black** to Alliser, who tells Jon he's making a mistake that insults everything the Night's Watch stands for. Jon says goodbye to **Samwell Tarly**, who gives him the dragonglass daggers, which are the only things that kill the undead White Walkers. **Gilly** spends time with the ailing **Maester Aemon**. Aegon was Aemon's little brother and became the king of the realm. He passes away and Samwell speaks for him before they burn the body. Alliser tells Samwell his list of friends is growing shorter.

Gilly is accosted by two rangers and Samwell warns them off, drawing his sword. The men beat him to the ground, but he stands and **Ghost**, the direwolf, defends them. The men flee and Samwell passes out. Later she cares for his wounds and makes him promise to take care of Little Sam if anything happened to her. They kiss, and then she climbs on top of him and they make love for the first time.

Quotes: Samwell Tarly: "He was the blood of the dragon, but now his fire has gone out."

The Prisoner

Theon brings **Sansa** breakfast in her room

and closes the open window. A snowstorm howls outside. She wakes and asks for his help, but Theon says to just do whatever Ramsey says or "he'll hurt you." But he already hurts her every night—she's locked in her room all day long, and then Ramsey visits at night. She asks Theon to send the signal from the broken tower so that Brienne of Tarth will come to her aid. She tries to convince him he's Theon. Later, **Ramsey** tells Sansa that Jon Snow has been made Lord Commander of the Night Watch. He also shows her the flayed body of the old woman who had visited her room.

Quotes: Sansa "It can't be any worse." Theon: "It can. It can always be worse."

The Stormcrows

To the north of Winterfell, **King Stannis Baratheon** has made his camp in the snowstorm. **Davos Seaworth** tells him that they are running out of food and horses and the **Stormcrows**, 500 sellswords, left in the night. Davos says they should retreat to Castle Black and wait, but Stannis wants to march as soon as possible. **Melisandre** says her visions have been true, but she needs Shireen's blood to ensure their victory. Stannis refuses.

Quotes: Davos Seaworth: "It's better to wait for the right time than risk everything." Stannis Baratheon: "This is the right time and I will risk everything because if I don't, we've lost. We march to victory, or we march to defeat. But we go forward. Only forward."

The Fighting Pits

Jorah Mormont and **Tyrion Lannister** are now slaves, being marched along the shoreline and the pyramids of Meereen are in the distance. At a slave auction, Jorah is sold Desperate to stay with Jorah, Tyrion says he's a great fighter as well and beats up the man holding his chain. The man buys Tyrion as well.

In bed with her lover **Daario Naharis**, **Daenerys Targaryen** is torn about marrying Hizdahr zo Loraq, a ploy to calm the city and solidify her hold over it.

Later, Jorah and Tyrion enter the games to earn a fight in the **Great Pit of Daznak** in

Meereen. Turns out the queen and **Hizdahr zo Loraq** are at today's fight. Jorah rushes out in a helmet and starts fighting while Tyrion works to free himself for a chain. After winning, he takes off his helmet, but Daenerys is disappointed. Jorah says he brought her a gift and Tyrion walks out.

Quotes: Daenerys Targaryen: "Get him out of my sight." Jorah Mormont: "Khaleesi, please, I just need a moment of your time. I brought you a gift." Tyrion Lannister: "It's true. He has." Daenerys Targaryen: "Who are you?" Tyrion Lannister: "I'm the gift. It's a pleasure to meet you, Your Grace. My name is Tyrion Lannister."

Notes: The slaver's stories about Jorah are not true, but close: he didn't slay Khal Drogo in single combat, but he did kill Drogo's bloodrider Qotho in **S01E09**.; Jorah wasn't the first through the breach at "Spike," attacking with his flaming sword—that was Thoros of Myr, attacking Pyke; and Jorah did not sell himself into slavery after being betrayed by his woman, but he did sell others into slavery and was sentenced to death for it by Ned Stark.

The King

In King's Landing, **Lady Olenna** demands the **High Sparrow** release Queen Margaery and her brother, Ser Loras Tyrell. He will not help, no matter what she offers him. On her way out of the Sept, she receives a message from Petyr Baelish.

King Tommen is furious that his queen is in captivity and there is nothing he can do about it. He shouts at **Cersei**, his mother, and says he's send in troops, but she tells him that's a sure way to get her killed. Cersei offers to speak to the High Sparrow on his behalf to free Margaery.

The Long Goodbye

In captivity in Dorne, **Jaime Lannister** is granted a few minutes to speak to **Myrcella**, his daughter. She's angry that he wants to take her away, no matter the reasons. She's in love with Trystane and wants to marry him. And in the cells, **Bronn** sings in the cell across from one that hold the three **Sand Snakes**. One of them, **Tyene**, tempts Bronn with her nudity, asking about the cut

86

on his arm. He starts to feel faint, and she says her dagger was laced with a poison called "**The Long Goodbye**." After he says she's the most beautiful woman in the world, she gives him the antidote.

Quotes: Myrcella Baratheon: "You looked different when I left. You had more hair." Jaime Lannister: "And more hands."

The Safest Place

Baelish tours his closed brothel, now decorated with scrawled versions of the seven-pointed star. The furniture is broken and paintings defaced. Lady Olenna is there to meet him—with the place closed, Baelish says he thought it was "the safest place" for them to meet. Olenna says that together they murdered a king, and their fates are intertwined. Baelish offers her a gift, the same gift he gave Cersei: a handsome young man.

In the **Sept of Baelor**, Cersei visits Queen Margaery, held in chains. The queen knows Cersei is behind this. On her way out, Cersei smiles and calls her "sister." She meets with the High Sparrow, who tells her there will be a trial for each. And then tells her that **Lancel** has told them of his unnatural relationship—with Cersei. They drag her away in custody and throw her into her own cell to await her own trial.

Quotes: High Sparrow: "Strip away the gold and ornaments, knock down the statues and pillars and this is what remains. What will we find when we strip away your finery?"

Notes: The Seven-Pointed Star is their holy book of sacred laws.

---------------------------------------—

Critique:

Karma. More of it would be appreciated on this show, but it's nice when it rears its' head, if only once in a while. Cersei Baratheon set this whole thing in motion, arming the Faith Militant and pushing the High Sparrow to exact justice on Ser Loras and Queen Margaery, but the problem with a powerful religious organization like that is it can find fault in anyone, even those who, behind the scenes, worked to give them the power they needed to enforce their doctrine. And the more people the Sparrows put in jails, the fewer there are out there with the power to stop them.

I like how Petyr Baelish continues to play both sides of the conflict between the Lannisters and the Tyrells, and in this episode even brings House Bolton and Sansa into it. He's known for playing the long game, as in having Lysa Arryn poison her husband and pin it on the Lannisters. But if he actually has feelings for Sansa—I can't really tell one way or the other—he's taking a big gamble she might end up dead.

In the east, I would have liked to have seen more of Valyria before Jorah and Tyrion moved on to Meereen. That ruined civilization and "the Doom" were fascinating, as were the Stone Men. But the slavers have moved on now and I'm surprised—in Jorah and Tyrion's very first pit fight, the queen happens to make an appearance. Frankly, I expected the show to drag that out much longer and make it much harder for Jorah to get his audience.

Oh, here's an update: seven episodes and no

word on Bran Stark and the three-eyed raven. It's been even longer since we've heard anything about Rickon Stark or the wildling Osha.

I recognize the "Hall of Faces" from the current Game of Thrones promotional materials. I'm watching these in the few days before the Season Six premiere, and I've seen the faces before in print and on promos. It was nice to see them introduced in the show—for some reason, I just expected that to be part of the marketing campaign.

Episode Notes:

The title of the episode refers to the gift offered by Petyr Baelish to both Cersei and Lady Olenna, along with Tyrion, the gift given to Daenerys by Jorah.

Nudity and Violence:

Flayed—Ramsey shows Sansa the flayed body of the old woman (15:45)

Tempted—In her jail cell, Tyene tempts Bronn with her boobs (41:10)

Stabbed—The fighting pits are full of cut

throats (48:33), blood sprays (49:35),

References:

Game of Thrones Wiki, several pages. http://gameofthrones.wikia.com/wiki/Game_of_T hrones_Wiki (accessed April 22, 2016)

HBO Game of Thrones Episode Synopsis. http://www.hbo.com/game-of-thrones/episodes/5/47-the-gift/synopsis.html (accessed April 22, 2016)

IMDB. http://www.imdb.com/title/tt3866846 (accessed April 22, 2016)

Episode Eight – "Hardhome"

Episode Number: S05E08
Original Air Date: May 31, 2015
Time: 61 minutes

Opening Credits

The animated map during the credits shows several important locations: **King's Landing**, **Winterfell**, the **Wall;** across the **Narrow Sea**, **Braavos** and **Meereen;** and far to the south, **Dorne**.

Service

Jorah Mormont and **Tyrion Lannister** stand before **Queen Daenerys Targaryen** and her translator, **Missandei**. Tyrion tells the story of how she was born, then tells her she's the last best hope to find a good leader for Westeros. She asks him to advise her—what should happen with Jorah? Tyrion says he's not a threat, but he cannot be part

93

of her leadership team when she moves on
Westeros.

Later, Daenerys and Tyrion share a drink
and discuss their fathers. He tells her she can never
take Westeros and the Iron Throne without the
support of the Houses, but she disagrees,
comparing the Houses to spokes on a wheel,
crushing others under it. "I'm going to break the
wheel."

Jorah goes back to the slaver and asks to
fight for him.

Quotes: Tyrion Lannister: "When I was a
young man I heard a story about a baby born
during the worst storm in living memory. She had
no wealth, no lands, no army, only a name and a
handful of supporters, most of whom probably
thought they could use that name to benefit
themselves. They kept her alive, moving her from
place to place, often hours ahead of the men who
had been sent to kill her. She was eventually sold
off to some warlord on the edge of the world and
that appeared to be that. And then a few years later,
the most well-informed person I knew told me that

this girl without wealth, lands, or armies had somehow acquired all 3 in a very short span of time, along with three dragons. He thought she was our best, last chance to build a better world. I thought you were worth meeting at the very least."

Lies

Arya Stark tells a tale about how she is **Lanna**, a girl who has saved up enough money to sell oysters in the local market. **Jaqen H'ghar** nods, saying Lanna will be a good servant of the Many-Faced God. He sends "Lanna" to Ragman Harbor. The next day, "Lanna" sells her oysters in the harbor, observing a **thin man** in the harbor who provides insurance to captains. He orders oysters from her.

Jaqen tells her that the man isn't paying out for those captains who don't return, leaving the families in ruins. Jaqen tells her that "Lanna" will return, learn all she can, and then give the thin man a "gift," handing her a small vial. Arya walks away, smiling. Her first assassination. The Waif says Arya isn't ready, but Jaqen is unconcerned. "It is all the same to the Many-Faced God."

Notes: Arya is learning to make up believable stories in which all the details are accurate.

Confess

In a cell in the Sept of Baelor, **Cersei Baratheon** awaits her trial. **Qyburn** arrives and tells her the charges: fornication, treason, incest, the murder of King Robert. He's concerned that Grand Master Pycelle now heads the Small Council and has called her uncle Kevan back from Casterly Rock to serve as the Hand of the King. King Tommen isn't eating or speaking to anyone. Qyburn asks her to confess to the High Sparrow.

Siege

Theon brings food to **Sansa Stark**, who waits for him. She wants to know why "Reek" told Ramsey, and Theon says he's helping her. "You wanted to escape. There is no escape." He tells her that he deserved everything that Ramsey did to him, listing off his crimes, but when he gets to Bran and Rickon says that he killed two other boys instead. Sansa is stunned—Bran and Rickon Stark are alive and on the run.

In the main hall, **Roose** and **Ramsey Bolton** meet with their war council. They say Stannis has 6,000 men, but more than half of those are mounted. Roose says they are prepared for a siege. Ramsey thinks they should ride out and hit them first, but Roose doesn't want to give up his defensive advantage. Ramsey says he doesn't need an army—just him and 20 good men.

Scared

At Castle Black, **Gilly** puts salve on **Samwell Tarly**'s wounds. He was punched and kicked in the face by two men accosting Gilly. **Olly** brings him food and asks why Jon Snow wants to save the wildlings. Far to the north, **Jon Snow** and a group of rangers, along with **Tormund** approach Hardhome, the main camp of wildlings, by boat. They land among a huge number of wildlings and are greeted by the **Lord of Bones**, the camp leader.

Tormund wants to hold a meeting of the elders, but the Lord of Bones says no and calls him a traitor. Tormund kills him and asks for a meeting. Jon Snow speaks to the elders, including Tormund, a woman named **Karsi** and a giant, **Wun Wun**. He offers the wildlings safe passage to the south and lands south of the Wall. Some agree, and they begin loading boats when the **Army of the Dead** sweeps down from the hillsides and attacks. They close the gates and wildlings swim toward the waiting ships.

Dead bash the gates and wildlings threaten to swamp the boats already on their way to the larger ships. Jon and the Night's Watch, along with Tormund and some of the other wildlings, drop back to the gates to defend the wildlings retreat. From the hillside, four white walkers on horseback watch the attack below. More dead swamp the camp, and Jon and the leader of the Thenns race to the meeting place, where the dragonglass was left behind. A white walker waits for them, and the Thenn fights him. The walker hits the Thenns axe, turning it to ice and shattering it, then killing the

Thenn. Jon fights him, blocking with **Longclaw**, the sword made of Valyrian steel, which does not shatter. He swings and destroys the creature.

Elsewhere, Tormund and Karsi fight the horde, and she is attacked and killed by a band of dead children. The dead pour over the hillside like water and overwhelm the walls, and Jon and the others run for the last boat. The White Walker leader, known as the Night King, walks out onto the dock and watches Jon and the others row away. He raises his arms, and all the dead around him stagger to their feet—his army has doubled in size.

Goofs: After Wun Wun walks into the water he completely disappears.

Notes: The leader of the walkers is called the Night King in HBO's official only synopsis, but the name isn't mentioned during the show. According to IMDB, it took three weeks, 50 stunt performers and 400 hundred extras to film the fight against the Army of the Dead. Also, the show's producers had to ask HBO for more money for CGI effects when their budget ran out during post-production.

--------------------------------------—

Critique:

Wow. Finally after five seasons, we get to see a huge battle between humans and the undead, and it really paid off. Lots of running around a screaming and being chased by zombies and former enemies banding together to resist the overwhelming force.

Watching the dead come pouring over the cliffs like water was chilling. I thought perhaps the white walkers were sacrificing them somehow, but then the dead staggered to their feet and resume their attack. I got chills when the Night King raised his hands and all those who had died in the attack slowly stood up and turned to watch Jon and the others row away. How do you defeat an army that is continually refilling its ranks? Can they be defeated?

Episode Notes:

The title of the episode refers to the wildling

camp where Jon goes to make peace and barely escapes with his life.

Nudity and Violence:

War—The war with the dead is not as graphic as it could have been, mostly because half of the combatants were already dead. Some blood did fly, but it was few and far between. Actually, one of the bloodiest deaths is that of the Lord of Bones when they first arrive at Hardhome—the blood seeps from his dead body.

References:

Game of Thrones Wiki, several pages. http://gameofthrones.wikia.com/wiki/Game_of_T hrones_Wiki (accessed April 21, 2016)

HBO Game of Thrones Episode Synopsis. http://www.hbo.com/game-of-thrones/episodes/5/48-hardhome/synopsis.html (accessed April 21, 2016)

IMDB. http://www.imdb.com/title/tt3866850 (accessed April 21, 2016)

Episode Nine – "The Dance of Dragons"

Episode Number: S05E09

Original Air Date: June 7, 2015

Time: 52 minutes

Opening Credits

The animated map during the credits shows several important locations: **King's Landing**, **Winterfell**, the **Wall;** across the **Narrow Sea**, **Braavos** and **Meereen;** and far to the south, **Dorne**.

Flames

To the Stannis camp north of Winterfell, **Melisandre** ventures out into the snowstorm as several tents catch fire. The next morning, **Davos Seaworth** tells **King Stannis Baratheon** that some twenty or so men snuck into the camp in the night unseen and set the fires, burning all the food and their siege weapons.

Davos says they should retreat to Castle Black, but Stannis has other ideas, looking at Melisandre and his wife **Selyse**. To the north, **Jon** returns to the **Wall** with hundreds of wildlings, and **Alliser Thorne** opens the gates. The wildlings file through **Castle Black** and pass into the south.

Dorne

In **Dorne**, **Jaime Lannister** joins **Prince Doran Martell**, **Ellaria Sand**, **Myrcella Lannister** and **Trystane Martell**. Jaime says he came to Dorne to take Myrcella home because of a threat—someone sent her necklace to Cersei. Myrcella says her necklace was stolen. Prince Doran says he doesn't want war and toasts King Tommen, but Ellaria pours out her drink.

Doran says that Myrcella can return to King's Landing, but Trystane will go with her and their engagement must stand. He also asks that Trystane be named to the Small Council, and Jaime accepts. Later, Doran insists Ellaria swear allegiance to him while the **Sand Snakes** stand nearby. She kneels and kisses his ring.

Quotes: Ellaria Sand: "No wonder you can't stand, you have no spine." Doran Martell: "You are mother to for of my nieces, girls I love very much. For their sake, I hope you live a long and happy life. Speak to me that way again and you won't."

Lies

Arya Stark continues to pose as the oyster merchant **Lanna**, selling her goods in Ragman Harbor. The thin man orders his oysters but she's distracted—**Lord Mace Tyrell** and his guard, **Ser Meryn** of the Kingsguard have arrived in Braavos. Ser Meryn is on her Kill List because she thinks he killed her "dancing" master, Syrio Forel. She follows them as Mace Tyrell chats with the representative of the **Iron Bank**. Later she follows Trant and his men to a brothel. Arya takes her food inside and sells to the whores and their customers and observes Trant, who likes his whores very young.

Offering

King Stannis Baratheon sends Davos to Castle Black for more supplies and horses. Later, Stannis comes to **Shireen**. He needs her help—and sends her to Melisandre, who burns her alive at the stake.

Quotes: Stannis Baratheon: "If you had to choose between Rhaenyra and Aegon, who'd you have chosen?" **Shireen Baratheon:** "I wouldn't have chosen either. It's all the choosing sides that made everything so horrible." **Stannis:** "Sometimes a person much choose. Sometimes... the world forces his hand. If a man knows what he is and remains true to himself, the choice is no choice at all. He must fulfill his destiny and become who he is meant to be. However much he may hate it."

Great Games

In Meereen, the **Great Games** begin in a massive coliseum. Thousands of spectators watch as men fight to the death in multiple matches.

Daenerys and **Tyrion** find the whole thing distasteful, but **Hizdahr zo Loraq** says it is a tradition that must continue.

In the second match, **Jorah** fights for his queen and wins. He grabs a spear and throws it at her, killing an assassin standing behind her. The killer was one of the Sons of the Harpy, and others stand from the crowds wearing their golden masks.

The **Sons of the Harpy** attack, killing dozens in the crowds and Hizdahr zo Loraq. Daario and Jorah protect Daenerys, getting them down onto the field, and Tyrion and Missandei follow, guarded by Unsullied. More Sons pour out onto the field, dozens of them, surrounding them.

Daenerys closes her eyes and hears the roar of dragons. **Drogon** lands, setting a dozen Sons afire while others flee. They throw spears, piercing the dragon's back, but Daenerys pulls one free and then climbs on Drogon's back, riding it. Together they fly away.

Location: The Great Games were filmed in a real stadium, the Plaza de Toros, located in Osuna, Spain. According to the "Scribbler in

Seville" website, these scenes were filmed over a twelve-day period in October 2014. Some 650 locals were used as extras.

-------------------------------------—

Critique:

Dragon time! Daenerys and Drogon are reunited just in time for him to show up and save her from being massacred by the vile Sons of the Harpy, who apparently just like to kill anyone. I thought they were the old masters rising up to take back their city, but they killed Hizdahr. Maybe they thought he was a traitor for marrying Daenerys. Anyway, I loved how they kept their masks hidden and didn't reveal themselves until Daenerys was distracted.

They swept through the coliseum, killing randomly, and managed to give the Unsullied a good challenge, probably just based on their sheer numbers. I have a practical question—where did they get all those masks? I'm thinking maybe "V" had them all shipped FedEx.

I kept waiting for Daenerys to yell or scream or somehow "call" to her children, but then I remembered they are still chained up in the catacombs, so it was Drogon who had to swoop in and save the day, or no one. Hizdahr bit it big time, Daario and Jorah were killing machines, as usual, Grey Worm is still home sicky, and Tyrion got in a few good licks as well, jumping out from behind a wooden beam and killing a dude. Nice!

Last question—is anyone else worried for Tyrion and the others? "Hey, Daenerys, you just flew off with the only thing keeping us alive!"

Elsewhere, nice to see Arya developing into a crafty assassin—she could be awesome, especially if she ever learns that face-swapping trick. Maybe she could ask John Travolta or Nick Cage. (Sorry, pop culture joke #2.)

Theon came clean about NOT killing Bran and Rickon, giving Sansa a little hope that she's not the last Stark. Oh, and for the record, we haven't seen anything to do with Bran or Rickon THIS WHOLE SEASON and this is episode nine. They better show up in the next episode or I'll be forced to pen a strongly-worded letter to my congressman.

Episode Notes:

The title of the episode refers to the book poor Shireen was reading. Sadly, it turned out to be her last. Also there were no scenes in King's Landing.

Nudity and Violence:

Games—The Great Games are a bloody affair: the quick man gets decapitated (40:45), Jorah stabs a dude in the chest (44:00), and Jorah stabs another dude (46:20). When the Sons of the Harpy appear, they slice a man's throat (47:05), another man's throat (47:10), stab a woman in the chest (47:11), an Unsullied is killed (47:35), Hizdahr is stabbed multiple times (47:40), Tyrion saves Missandei (48:15), an Unsullied gets stabbed (48:30), and one of the Sons gets stabbed (49:40).

References:

Game of Thrones Wiki, several pages.
http://gameofthrones.wikia.com/wiki/Game_of_T

hrones_Wiki (accessed April 22, 2016)

HBO Game of Thrones Episode Synopsis.
http://www.hbo.com/game-of-thrones/episodes/5/49-the-dance-of-dragons/synopsis.html (accessed April 22, 2016)

IMDB.
http://www.imdb.com/title/tt3866826 (accessed April 22, 2016)

Scribbler in Seville.
http://scribblerinseville.com/game-of-thrones-season-5-osuna-the-fighting-pit-of-meereen/ (accessed April 22, 2016)

Episode Ten – "Mother's Mercy"

Episode Number: S05E10
Original Air Date: June 14, 2015
Time: 60 minutes

Opening Credits

The animated map during the credits shows several important locations: **King's Landing**, **Winterfell**, the **Wall;** across the **Narrow Sea**, **Braavos** and **Meereen;** and far to the south, **Dorne**.

Deserters

To the Stannis camp north of Winterfell, **Melisandre** tells **King Stannis Baratheon** that the Lord of Light has stopped the snowstorm and cleared the way for Stannis to attack Winterfell. But he gets bad news—nearly half of his army has deserted in the night, disgusted with his sacrifice of his own daughter. In the woods, he finds his wife

Selyse, who has hung herself. Melisandre rides away from camp, and Stannis orders the men to Winterfell.

In Winterfell, they prepare for the approaching army. Sansa picks the lock on her door and leaves, climbing the tower. From outside the walls, Pod sees the Stannis army approaching and tells Brienne, who is observing Winterfell from a distance. She's still watching for the light in the broken tower but misses it when Sansa finally lights it.

Maester

Jon Snow tells **Samwell Tarly** about the **Night King** raising his hands and reanimating all the dead at Hardhome. Samwell figures out why Jon could kill a white walker with **Longclaw**, his sword—it's Valyrian steel. Samwell asks to go to Oldtown with Gilly to become a maester, now that Maester Aemon is dead, and Jon gives him permission to leave.

March on Winterfell

Roose Bolton and his army ride out to meet them in the field and it's a massacre. Stannis is barely alive when Brienne of Tarth finds him. She asks him about the shadow that killed Renly and if he used some sort of blood magic. He admits he did, and she kills him.

Ramsey is having the time of his life, killing as many Stannis men as he can find. Sansa is running around the battlements looking for a way out and is stopped by Myranda and Theon.

Myranda tries to shoot Sansa but Theon throws her over a railing and her head smashes on the courtyard below. Hearing the army returning, Theon and Sansa jump from the walls.

Quotes: Stannis Baratheon: "Bolton has women fighting for him?" Brienne of Tarth: "I don't fight for the Boltons. I'm Brienne of Tarth. I was Kingsguard to Renly Baratheon. I was there when he was murdered by a shadow with your face. You murdered him with blood magic?" Stannis Baratheon: "I did." Brienne of Tarth: "In the name of Renly of House Baratheon, First of His Name,

Rightful King of the Andals and the First Men, Lord of the Seven Kingdoms and Protector of the Realm, I, Brienne of Tarth, sentence you to die. Do you have any last words?" Stannis Baratheon: "Go on, do your duty."

Notes: With the death of Stannis, there is only one legitimate known person with Baratheon blood left in House Baratheon: Gendry, the armorers apprentice. It is possible that other bastards of King Robert survived Joffrey's purge. Renly and Stannis had no other children, and Tommen is a Baratheon in name only.

Hall of Faces

In Braavos, **Ser Trant** is beating three young girls with a switch. Two of them cry out but the third does not. She parts her hair and is unfamiliar to us. Trant says he has his work cut out for him and dismisses the other two.

He punches her in the belly and she doubles over. She changes faces and is **Arya Stark**, lunging at him with a knife. She stabs him in one eye, then the other, then in the chest many times. She tells him why she is killing him, then kills him.

Back in the **Hall of Faces**, Arya returns the face of the young girl. **Jaqen** and the **Waif** are there, and Jaqen tells Arya she's taken the wrong life. He says only death can pay for a life and swallows poison, falling dead. Arya is furious but Jaqen walks up behind her. She sees it's a trick and pulls more faces off the dead man, face after face, until she uncovers her own. After a moment, she goes blind.

Snakes

In Dorne, **Prince Doran Martell**, **Ellaria Sand** and the **Sand Snakes** see **Jaime Lannister**, **Myrcella Lannister, Trystane Martell** and **Bronn** off at the docks for their return to King's Landing. Ellaria kisses Myrcella, and Bronn says a reluctant goodbye to **Tyene**, one of the snakes. Jaime gives the necklace back to Myrcella and starts to tell her that he's her father, but she already knew. She starts to bleed from the nose—she's been poisoned with "The Long Farewell." Ellaria starts to bleed from the nose as well and takes the antidote.

The Mountains

Tyrion Lannister is waiting in Daenearys' chambers with **Jorah** and **Daario** when **Gray Worm** and **Missandei** enter. He's recovered from his wounds. Daario says that he and Jorah need to go to find Daenerys, and Tyrion, Missandei and Gray Worm should stay and govern Meereen in her stead. Later, Lord Varys arrives as Tyrion watches Jorah and Daario ride off.

High in distant mountains, **Daenerys** asks **Drogon** to return her to Meereen. He's injured and tired. She tries to ride him but he bucks her off. She goes off searching for food and is surrounded by hundreds of horsemen of the Dothraki.

Quotes: Lord Varys: "Hello old friend. I thought we're so happy together until you abandon me." Tyrion Lannister: "I suppose there's no point ask how you find me." Lord Varys: "The bird see in the west, the bird see in the east. If one knows how to listen. They tell me that you already found favor with the mother of dragons." Tyrion Lannister:

"Well. She did not execute me. So that's a promising start. Now the heroes are off to find her. And I'm stuck here. Trying to placate a city in a brink of civil war. I will need advice from how to command." Lord Varys: "Information is the key. You need to learn your enemy's strength and strategies. You need to learn which of your friends are not your friends." Tyrion Lannister: "If only I knew someone with a vast network of spies." Lord Varys: "If only. A grand old city. Choking of violence, corruption and deceit... Who could possibly have any experience of managing such a massive ungainly beast?" Tyrion Lannister: "I did miss you." Lord Varys: "Oh I know."

Shame

Cersei is still in her prison cell and the guard tells her to confess. She it taken before the **High Sparrow** and confesses to a relationship with Lancel Lannister. The High Sparrow offers her a trial but allows her to return to the Red Keep to see her son. First she must atone for her sins—she is stripped naked and washed, and her hair is cut short.

Cersei is then taken out onto the Sept of Baelor and makes her "walk of atonement," paraded naked through the streets. The woman walking with her calls out "shame" over and over again while she rings a bell. The crowd shouts at her, calling her names and mocking her. Once she gets to the Red Keep and is protected by the Gold Cloaks, **Qyburn** covers her. He presents the newest member of the Kingsguard—Ser Gregor "The Mountain" Clegane.

Notes: This is the first time we see Cersei Lannister nude.

Castle Black

Davos Seaworth pleads with Jon Snow to send men or the wildlings to assist Stannis and his troops, not knowing they've already all been wiped out. Melisandre rides through the gates, telling them that all of them are dead. Later, Jon reads messages when **Olly** calls him—a wildling has come in, reporting that he knows the location of Benjen Stark, Jon's uncle and a ranger who was lost and presumed dead in the north. Alliser walks Jon out, who looks for the wildling but instead finds a sign that reads "traitor."

Alliser stabs Jon in the chest, then another ranger, and several more. He falls to the ground, and Olly steps up and stabs him as well. As they stab him, they each say "For the Watch." Jon falls to the ground and blood seeps from him in all directions.

--------------------------------------—

Critique:

Wow. Okay, lots of stuff happened during this final episode of season five, so let's unpack it.

Starting with Daenerys, she's stranded in a random distant location "to the north," which isn't saying much. She's captured by horsemen and Drogon is hurt. I'm assuming she dropped her ring so that someone could find her, but I'm always suspicious about searchers finding one item in a trampled field like that, although Aragorn did it. "Not idly do the leaves of Lothlorien fall." I guess if he can do it, Jorah and Daario together might spot it.

Blinding Arya is an interesting choice, but I doubt it will last. She got to cross another name off her list, and we got to see her change faces at least once, which was cool. We got to see some more of the mechanics of the face switching—evidently they just keep all the faces in their big bank of faces and you can check them out if you want. It's like a library, I guess. What's the late fee on a face, I wonder?

I like that Tyrion's found a place in the east. I hope he's better at running Meereen than Daenerys was—at least he's got Lord Varys to help.

I KNEW that Ellaria had poisoned the Lannister girl. I expected her to die before Jaime could tell her the truth about her parentage, and as soon as he launched into his conversation, filled with fits and starts, I kept watching for her vision to blur. They went with the bloody nose, though, and it was better because we're just looking at her and it starts and you know. I like that both she and Ellaria were poisoned and both started bleeding from the nose at the same time—but only one of them had the antidote. Nice.

Stannis and all of his men and machinations and murder come to absolutely nothing. I'm thinking those sellswords and the other men who "deserted" in the middle of the night—after watching Stannis burn his own daughter to death—had the right idea.

Jon Snow. You can't screw everyone over and then expect them to line up behind you. He knew Alliser was bad, and had a whole crew of folks behind him that hated Jon. Thankfully Samwell and Gilly are already gone.

Episode Notes:

The title of the episode refers to the Mother, one of the aspects of the Faith of the Seven. For the record, we went the entire season without any word on Bran or Rickon Stark. Bran we last saw in **S04E10** when he talked to the three-eyed raven under the weirwood tree. We haven't seen Rickon since Osha took him off to find the Last Hearth in **S03E09**, the same episode that saw the deaths of

Robb and Catelyn Stark. And, according to IMDB, the Iron Throne is not shown during the entire season.

Nudity and Violence:

Knifed—Stannis kills a guy with a knife to the neck (17:02)

Tossed—Myranda takes a header into some cobblestones (21:35)

Stabbed—Arya crosses Trant off her list with lots of stabby stab stabbing (24:10) and then she cuts his throat (25:40)

Shamed—Cersei's nude and washed roughly and paraded through the streets (47:50) It's an extended scene of full nudity that goes on and on for several minutes. Apparently they used a body double and added Lena Headey's face digitally. During the walk we also see another woman naked (52:44), a man strips, showing his cock (53:02), and another man flashes his cock (53:30).

References:

Game of Thrones Wiki, several pages. http://gameofthrones.wikia.com/wiki/Game_of_Thrones_Wiki (accessed April 22, 2016)

HBO Game of Thrones Episode Synopsis.http://www.hbo.com/game-of-thrones/episodes/5/50-mothers-mercy/synopsis.html (accessed April 22, 2016)

IMDB. http://www.imdb.com/title/tt3866862 (accessed April 22, 2016)

Game of Thrones: A Binge Guide to Season 5

Copyright © 2016, 2019 by Greg Enslen

Published in the United States of America

For more information, please see the author's website at **www.gregenslen.com**.

Cover photo: "Hohenzollern Castle in Stuttgart, Germany"

by Jim Trodel/Flickr, used under CC BY / Altered from original

About the Author

Greg Enslen is an Ohio author and columnist. He's written and published eighteen books, including five fiction titles, several non-fiction guides and four collections of newspaper columns. Several are available through Gypsy Publications of Troy, Ohio. To receive updates on upcoming titles, sneak previews and appearances, subscribe to Email Goodies. For more information, please see his **Amazon Author Page** or visit his **Facebook fan page**. Find out more **www.gregenslen.com**.

Books by Greg Enslen

All titles are available on Kindle:

Fiction

Black Bird

The Ghost of Blackwood Lane

The 9/11 Machine

Frank Harper Mysteries

A Field of Red

Black Ice

Guide Series

A Field Guide to Facebook

A Viewer's Guide to Suits for Season 1

A Viewer's Guide to Suits for Season 2

A Viewer's Guide to Suits for Season 3

Game of Thrones: A Binge Guide for Season 1

Game of Thrones: A Binge Guide for Season 2

Game of Thrones: A Binge Guide for Season 3

Game of Thrones: A Binge Guide to Season 5

Game of Thrones: A Binge Guide for Season 4
Game of Thrones: A Binge Guide for Season 5

Newspaper Column Collections

"Tipp Talk" Newspaper Column Collections
for years 2010, 2011, 2012, and 2013

Can I Ask A Favor?

Thank you for reading this book - I hope you enjoyed it. If you enjoyed this book, found it useful or otherwise then I'd really appreciate it if you would post a short review on Amazon. If you could, take a few minutes out to write a review of this book on **Amazon**, **Goodreads**, Facebook or any other place you feel like sharing.

If you'd like to leave a review for one of my books, please visit the link below: http://bit.ly/geauthor Reviews are the best way readers discover new books. And, believe it or not, the sheer number of Amazon reviews affects how Amazon lists book titles. So swing over there and jot down a couple of sentences. Good or bad, every review helps increase the "social buzz" of the book. I would truly appreciate it.

— Greg Enslen

Made in the USA
Monee, IL
02 September 2021